Rocks a

Heather Hammonds

Contents

My Rock Collection

This is my **rock collection**.
I have big rocks
and little rocks.

I have some rocks
from the garden.
I keep my rocks in a box.
I have some rocks
from a shop, too.

Rocks Everywhere

Rocks are all around us.
There are many rocks
in this river.

These big mountains
are made of rock.

Big rocks are sometimes called **boulders**.

This old rock looks
like a wave.
People come to look
at the rock.

Everyone likes
to look at this huge rock.
It looks red
as the sun goes down.

Rocks and Earth

A lot of Earth
is made of rock.
The land is made of rock.

There is rock under the sea.

There is rock
inside Earth, too.

Hot Rock

Some of the rock inside Earth is very hot. Sometimes the hot rock comes out of the earth.

The hot rock looks like this when it is cold.

Looking at Rocks

You can see lots of rocks at a **museum**.

This museum has
a big rock collection.
Everyone can see the rocks.

Make a Rock Collection

You can make
a rock collection.
You will need:

box

My Rocks

rocks

magnifying glass

- Ask your Mom or Dad to help you find some rocks.

- Keep the rocks in the box.

- Show the rocks to your friends.

My Rocks

Glossary

boulders

rock

collection

museum